The Vocation and Mission

of

Joseph and Mary

Paul Molinari SJ

Anne Hennessy CSJ

VERITAS

First published 1992 by
Veritas Publications
7-8 Lower Abbey Street
Dublin 1

ISBN 1 85390 149 0

British Library Cataloguing
in Publication Data.
A catalogue record for
this book is available
from the British Library.

Cover design: Centraline Creative, Dublin
Printed in the Republic of Ireland
by Criterion Press Ltd, Dublin

Contents

We dedicate this book to the many married people
who have been a source of inspiration for us.

Foreword

When a Christian lives in Galilee for any length of time something takes place within the person. In a subtle yet deep way one is 'touched' by the surroundings: the sky and the landscape, the villages and the olive groves, the water of the Sea of Gennesaret and the hills of Upper Galilee, the fishermen and the farmers – everything speaks to the mind and the heart of the person who is open to the powerful attraction of the land of Jesus.

We have spent months at a time, which have now accumulated into years, living on the shores of the Sea of Galilee. It is here that we have perceived the experiences of Jesus' family, Joseph and Mary, more clearly. We have pondered their lives, prayerfully reflecting on the Gospel passages which give the accounts of how they became progressively aware of their vocation and mission. We have been helped by encounters with village people whose families have lived for generations in the land of Israel, and who have shared with us some of their customs, traditions, attitudes and values. We have also put at the service of our contemplative experiences in Galilee the works of biblical scholars and of sociologists of first-century Palestine.

Several convictions have guided our reflections: While respecting and incorporating the contributions of scientific exegesis to the literary and theological formation of the gospels, we have approached the texts as they stand, that is, as they have been proclaimed, understood and artistically expressed within the Christian community through the centuries.

We recognise and accept the scholarly consensus that the first chapters of Matthew and Luke, usually called the Infancy Narratives, have some details and theological themes in common but are two distinct accounts. We do not seek to reconcile the two into a cohesive story-line but to draw from each account insights into the mission which God gave to Mary and Joseph.

We view the Gospels as the fruit of the active nurturing of a remembering community in which each eye-witness contributed his or her personal experiences with Christ the Lord. We presume that the texts redacted by Luke and to a lesser extent by Matthew speak of personal experiences which were graciously shared, directly or indirectly, by Mary and Joseph.

We approach the annunciations to both Joseph and Mary not as single events but as growth processes of deeply spiritual people living ordinary lives in a first-century Jewish village. Furthermore, since they were Israelites steeped in the religious traditions and practices of their people, they were very familiar with the stories of the religious heroes and heroines of their tradition. Therefore their own histories predictably incorporate expressions from the stories of such people as Abraham, Moses, Jeremiah and Samuel, which by the first century had acquired specific theological meaning.

Finally, from our contemplative reading of the Infancy Narratives, it becomes evident that although the Matthean community emphasised the annunciation to and vocation of Joseph, and the Lukan community focused on Mary, at a certain point both traditions began to consider Joseph and Mary together: '...he (Joseph) took his wife...' (Mt 1:24); and '...Joseph also went up ... to be enrolled with Mary...' (Lk 2:5). Their lives and missions were intertwined. When Joseph took Mary into his home and the birth of the child was imminent, they formed a family unit and 'the parents of Jesus' acted in concert.

It is our hope that these reflections on the stories of the vocation and mission of Joseph and Mary which have been preserved by the first Christian communities will help prayerful readers to become more aware of God's action in them as they respond to their own vocations.

Paul Molinari SJ   Anne Hennessy CSJ

'Living Water' — Tabgha
Tiberias (ISRAEL)
Feasts of St Joseph and the
Annunciation
19&25 March 1992

1

The Vocation of Joseph

Very little is known about Joseph because the gospels convey so little about him as a person. Still less is said about his vocation. Yet Joseph lived in a first-century Jewish village society which was steeped in its biblical heritage. The story of the people of Israel, the vocations of the patriarchs and prophets, as well as the psalms, formed the mind and heart of the people and shaped their milieu. Looking at the portrait of Joseph in the Infancy Narratives, against this socio-religious background, may reveal something of the richness of his personality and the development of his vocation.

> When his mother Mary had been betrothed to Joseph ... a just man ... (Mt 1:18-19).[1]

The just person is portrayed in the psalms as having three sets of qualities. He is noted for his generosity: giving freely, especially to the poor, and lending money liberally and without taking interest (Ps 112:5a, 9a; 37:21b, 26; 15:5a). He is also known for prudence in verbal communication: not only does he avoid sins of the tongue (Ps 15:3), he utters wisdom and justice (Ps 37:30).[2] The just person has a steady heart; he is steadfast and firm (Ps 112:7b-8a); he is holy and serious. The root of this compendium of virtue is the Law: 'the Law of his God is in his heart' (Ps 37:31), and it is in the Law that he takes delight (Ps 1:2).

Joseph lived in a small Jewish village in first-century Galilee. As in any peasant village, people lived in closely-knit groups and knew each other's behaviour well.[3] His neighbours would have known Joseph's justice first-hand. Because he was a builder, Joseph had a breadth of experience beyond that of other tradesmen or farmers. Carpenters and masons travelled from village to village, and those in the region of Nazareth undoubtedly went to Sepphoris, the cosmopolitan administrative centre of Galilee where there were many construction projects throughout the first century.[4] Joseph would have had an opportunity to observe other people's religiosity as well as to practise his own religious ideals in a variety of circumstances.

Joseph's home and his village were marked by the practices of Judaism as prescribed in the Torah;[5] in fact, scholars tell us that the Talmud praises builders for their knowledge of Torah. Training in the Law began at an early age, and fathers were responsible for teaching their children by word and example. Instruction obviously began with the greatest of the commandments: '... you shall love the Lord your God with all your heart, and with all your soul, and with all your might' (Dt 6:5). God's saving kindness to his people was also an important lesson. According to the instructions in Exodus, at each Passover the father of the family explained to the children that the feast they were celebrating recalled what God had done for his people when he brought them out of the slavery of Egypt: 'And you shall tell your son on that day "It is because of what the Lord did for me when I came

11

out of Egypt"' (Ex 13:8). The ideals of Covenant spirituality formed the heart of the pious Jew: humble gratitude for God's graciousness and obedience to his Law.

The religious practices of Jewish home life – prayers, teaching, purifications, dietary laws, fasts and feasts – were supplemented by the community gathering in the local synagogue. Here the villagers assembled not only or even primarily for prayer, but for the reading, study, discussion and interpretation of the Law and the Prophets. As he grew to adulthood and prepared for marriage, Joseph the just man undoubtedly became more and more a part of the social and religious life which revolved around his local synagogue. He shared the concerns and expectations of his people who lived in a land occupied by the Romans. They waited for spiritual, political and social freedom: they longed for the coming of the Messiah.

Joseph the just man was deeply devoted to the Law of God as this was expressed and interpreted in his religion. Although his moral security was rooted in fulfilling what his religion told him and in being loyal to a God of Law, Joseph, the simple pious Jew, knew the difference between fidelity to God and mere observance of the Law.[6] Still, it must have been a shock for someone who knew God within the context of the Law to encounter the Spirit who 'breaks the law'! However, like the holy people of his tradition, when the God-who-goes-beyond-the-Law called him, Joseph responded, however many or probing were the questions of his steadfast heart.

Joseph, the just man of his tradition, knew the

promise made to virtuous people:

> Your wife will be like a fruitful vine
> within your house;
> your children will be like olive shoots
> around your table.
> Lo, thus shall the man be blessed
> who fears the Lord. (Ps 128:3-4)

This promise of God formed Joseph's expectations. Obviously as a young man he looked forward to having a wife who would give him a large family, a great and noble posterity. Other men may have appreciated Mary or been attracted to her because of some quality. Yet, without being aware of what God was doing in him, Joseph's refinement enabled him to sense and to appreciate the exquisite qualities of Mary. Similarly, it was Joseph who had that disposit- ion of heart which enabled Mary to respond to him and to be at ease with him. There was a correspondence, a mutuality between them which was the basis for their betrothal.

In first-century society marriages were arranged as family alliances; however, the marriage would not take place without some kind of consent on the part of the young girl. In fact, we are told by Jewish documents that it was not the man who set his bride apart, who betrothed her to himself. On the contrary, young girls who had reached about thirteen years took an active part in the marriage. The bride herself (not the responsible male relative) accepted the token which stood for the dowry.[7] Mary's active consent tells us that there must have been a spiritual affinity between herself and Joseph.

> ...before they came together she was found to be with child of the Holy Spirit... (Mt 1:18)

Joseph the builder was betrothed, but something strange happened. What had taken place in Mary affected Joseph and confronted him with a situation that was totally 'alien'. How was it possible that someone of Mary's spiritual refinement, someone with whom Joseph the just man had such a deep bond 'was found to be with child'? Joseph's inner suffering seared his soul and challenged his justice to the core. Like Mary who was 'greatly troubled' (Lk 1:29), so Joseph was puzzled and concerned. Instinctively he must have turned to God: '...deliver me for the sake of thy steadfast love' (Ps 6: 3-4), because both Joseph and his beloved, at the mercy of their fellow religionists in a closed village society, must have known the pain of being despised by 'good' people who had not been called beyond human and divine laws.

Joseph's suffering came not only from his perplexity but also from his dilemma: How was he to act in such circumstances? The time between the ceremony of betrothal and their living together was considered as uniting the couple. They were truly bound, and because a woman's honour was the responsibility of her husband, the consequences of Mary's vocation rested on Joseph.[8]

...and her husband Joseph...unwilling to put her to shame, resolved to send her away quietly (Mt 1:19).

Joseph was a 'good' person; a person of integrity in whom personal uprightness was balanced with compassion for human realities. He brought these qualities to the painful situation in which he found himself.

There were two formalities which constituted the establishment of a marriage: the exchange of consent and the taking of the bride into the groom's family home. Religiously and legally the mutual consent to marry was binding. Therefore Mary's condition reflected on both of them.

The first reaction of Joseph and of their society would have been to assign guilt in a situation of this kind. Was Mary a perpetrator or a victim? Because holiness of a Jew extends to one's surroundings, the 'just man' could not accept into his home someone who was 'unholy' or 'guilty'. Therefore, Joseph's natural reaction was to divorce Mary, that is, to break the contract that united them. Not only the closeness of village society, but also the form of divorce (delivering a writ to the woman or her representative in front of two witnesses) prevented privacy or secrecy. And so Joseph's resolve to break their marriage 'quietly' is usually understood to mean that he would not publicly accuse Mary, would not presume her guilty, would not instigate a formal inquiry into her behaviour.[9]

> But as he considered this, behold, an angel of
> the Lord appeared to him in a dream, saying,
> 'Joseph, son of David... ' (Mt 1:20).

The description of God's intervention in Joseph's
life has many characteristics of the Old Testament
vocation stories of the Patriarchs and Prophets. An
angel of the Lord appeared to Joseph in a dream:
'(the Lord) provides for his beloved as they sleep'
(Ps 127:2,JB). Angelic visitations and dreams are
typically biblical ways of describing God's presence
among human beings and divine communications
to those chosen for a special mission.[10]

The divine intervention is both awesome and
frightening. It is understood as a personal
imperative; the person is called by name. When
Moses saw the burning bush which was on fire but
was not consumed and went forward to look at the
strange sight, he heard the voice of God calling
him: 'Moses, Moses!' (Ex 3:4). He realised then that
he was in the presence of the God of his ancestors.
When Samuel, repeatedly responding to a voice
which called him by name, came to realise that it
was God who was calling to him, he said, 'Speak,
Lord, for thy servant hears' (1 S 3:10). So also,
when Joseph was searching and heard himself
called by name, 'Joseph, Son of David', he realised
that it was God himself who was there and who
had something to convey to him.

> ...do not be afraid to take Mary your wife, for
> that which is conceived in her is of the Holy
> Spirit (Mt 1:20).

Such words of reassurance as 'do not be afraid' are found in all the accounts of the calls of patriarchs and prophets. They are usually associated with the promise of God's 'being with' the person chosen for a mission. The task to be accomplished, being difficult and beyond human capacities, demanded that the Giver of the mission be at the side of the person called. If the person relied on God, he would see to it that the mission would be accomplished successfully. Hence the words of reassurance dispel hesitation, doubt and reluctance: 'do not be afraid to take Mary your wife'.

Joseph's mission was to be entrusted with Mary and her child. He was to take her as his wife. God not only eased Joseph's doubts about Mary, God also revealed the divine plan: her child was conceived of the Holy Spirit. And therefore, a second aspect of Joseph's mission was made known: he was called to empty himself of the natural desire for parenthood. He was not to be the child's father. Mary was the true mother, but Joseph was called to step aside, to hand over to the Lord his potential fatherhood. Joseph's vocation was not only to be at Mary's side with practical and affectionate support but to act as if he were Jesus' father. Joseph's role was to be the shadow of God the Father.

> She will give birth to a son and you must
> name him Jesus ... (Mt 1:21, JB).

Mary is the mother who will bring forth Jesus, the Son of God, into the world. Joseph will be at her

17

side to give her support and to care for her: he will be there to protect the child, not only as a human father does for his children, but also to give this unique child the security of a 'family' which is officially acknowledged by the society that surrounds them. No one has to know how the child was conceived and how they, Joseph and Mary, had enabled God to act by responding to their vocations to virginity.

In that society it was the duty and the responsibility of the father to name the child; this act was his acknowledgement of paternity. Joseph, who accepted fully his own vocation as shadow of the Father will, when the time comes, give to the child the name that the Heavenly Father wants to be given to him. And so Joseph is told the name he is to give the child that Mary is carrying without his having taken any part in its conception. There is the divine imperative: '...you must name him'. That is, Joseph is to assume the public and legal role of fatherhood by giving the name.[11] However, the child's name is not Joseph's choice but God's. It is well known that in Jewish tradition as in several other cultures the name is descriptive of personality and role in life. Sometimes parents chose a child's name even before its conception to indicate their hope for the role and the manner in which the person would develop throughout life. The name Joseph is to give Mary's child, however, is the name by which the Father knows him: Jesus, in Hebrew, 'Yahweh saves'. The Father knows Jesus as the One who will save, and this knowledge is revealed to Joseph: '...you must name him Jesus, because he is the one who is to save his people from their sins' (Mt 1:21, JB).

The name Jesus here takes on its own destiny. It is a statement of who Jesus will be, a declaration of his life and mission. At the same time the revelation of Jesus' name to Joseph broadens his understanding of his own vocation to act as father. Joseph's acceptance of this formulation of his mission is one stage in his growing awareness of who the child is and what Joseph's own role will be: the child he was to care for as father, while not being its father, was the One foreshadowed by the prophets as Saviour/Messiah.

> When Joseph woke up he did what the angel of the Lord had told him to do: he took his wife to his home and, though he had not had intercourse with her, she gave birth to a son; and he named him Jesus (Mt 1:24, JB).

The prompt response given by Joseph to the Lord's word puts him in line with other important biblical figures. Do we not find in Genesis (12:4) 'So Abram went as the Lord had told him'? Once the light of God enters the heart, anxiety, doubts and perplexities are all set aside. Joseph was truly the just man, obedient to God and not only to the law. Thus he was ready to begin a form of life which was completely new. He was to take Mary his wife and to act as her spouse, and yet not to have marital relations with her. Theirs was to be a new kind of relationship in which two minds and two hearts are mutually supportive in responding to the plan of God in which their

19

respective vocations are situated.[12]

When Joseph took Mary into his home under these terms, he indicated the acceptance of his vocation: his relationship with Mary and with her Son. Their marriage was one that stood against common social practice: they had a completely different kind of communication born of their unique vocations.

Just as Mary had responded to the Divine Plan, '...let be to me according to your word' (Lk 1:38), so Joseph acted according to what he had been told. Each accepted a personal vocation. Because Mary the virgin accepted hers, Joseph whose heart had been so open to the divine, that is, so virginal, accepted the vocation to a life of virginity and took Mary, with all the mystery of her maternity, into his home to act as a husband and father while being a virgin.[13]

They both knew the importance of paternity to those in their Jewish tradition: 'Lo, sons are a heritage from the Lord, the fruit of the womb a reward. Like arrows in the hand of a warrior are the sons of one's youth. Happy is the man who has his quiver full of them!' (Ps 127:3-5) Yet Joseph bowed to the Lord and agreed to take on all the outward responsibilities of a husband and a father without being either 'in totum'. He surrendered to the One whose 'ways are not our ways' (Is 55:9). The mutuality, the 'togetherness', of this marriage was totally rooted in Joseph's and Mary's absolute docility to God and in their sharing a disposition of hearts: God's will be done.

The Vocation of Mary

The Old Testament counterpart to the masculine image of the just man is the portrait of the 'good wife' in the Book of Proverbs (31:10-27). The ideal woman is a person of foresight, strength, dignity and wisdom. For most first-century Jewish women this ideal was lived out in small villages where they fulfilled daily routine tasks and customs rooted in the Law deriving from the Covenant.

As is well known, girls did not normally have formal schooling, yet they were brought up from an early age to develop a sense of responsibility. They were trained to assume the demanding tasks of wife and mother. Every good mother would see to it that her daughters grew up striving to meet the ideals and being proficient in the duties of a good Jewish wife and mother as described in Scripture and the Torah. Women were responsible for drawing water from the well, for preparing and baking the bread, for spinning and weaving — three major tasks whose proper accomplishment entailed much hard work, endurance, patience and attentiveness. It is evident that fulfilling these tasks required hours of diligence. The bread-making alone involved grinding grain with a mortar or a handmill made of two stones, mixing, kneading, then gathering wood for the fire and tending it, and, finally, watching the baking. Spinning and weaving began with the woman using distaff and spindle to make thread from the raw wool. Then she had to weave the yarn into cloth on a hand loom. Drawing water meant going to the village spring or well where all the women of the village assembled early in the morning to exchange news and to watch the children. It was in such contexts that relationships among the women developed.[1]

Mary grew humanly, affectively and spiritually in such a situation in which women did not have a public role but exercised great influence in the shaping of the family and the growth of the children. In this atmosphere every girl was effectively prepared for marriage and mother-hood.[2] Even though marriages were substantially arranged by the parents (the father of the future bridegroom approached the parents of the possible future wife for his son), in Galilean circles the betrothal did not take place unless the girl, who had to be about thirteen years old to be considered a partner, also gave her consent.[3]

It was in such a context that Mary progressively experienced God manifesting himself to her in a very personal and unique manner. Mary came to perceive clearly that God was near her, that God was whispering something precious to her, that God was speaking to her through his messenger, Gabriel. The climax of this growing interaction between God and herself was the conception of Jesus, the long-awaited Messiah, the Son of God who became flesh in her. Through the angel God brought about in Mary the keen perception of what he was about to do as a consequence of her constant openness and docility to the gentle promptings which he had constantly brought about in her as she was growing as a girl and a young woman in an ordinary situation in a less-than-ordinary village called Nazareth of Galilee.[4]

> In the sixth month the angel Gabriel was sent from God to a city in Galilee named Nazareth, to a virgin betrothed to a man whose name was Joseph, of the house of David, and the virgin's name was Mary (Luke 1:26-7).

'In the sixth month...'
The indication of the precise time of the event Mary shared is not given in terms of the calendar but in reference to a specific moment of salvation history. It is the time when the message of the prophets is about to find fulfilment in the conception of the last and greatest of the prophets, John the Baptist: 'Truly I say to you, among those born of women there has risen no one greater than John the Baptist...' (Mt 11:11). This time reference indicates a fundamental attitude of Mary: she saw history in terms of God's saving action, his love for his people. We are told that in the sixth month of Elizabeth's pregnancy God acted very powerfully in the heart of a young woman who was a virgin, that is, who was totally open to God.

'...to a city in Galilee named Nazareth...'
Throughout the history of his Chosen People, God had selected persons from different places to play specific roles in this salvific action. This time the

divine attention was focused on that part of Israel called Galilee; God centred his attention on a given area of the land, a tiny village off the beaten track which was regarded even then with contempt. Nazareth nestles in a basin-like range of hills which cut it off from the major trade routes through the valleys of Esdralon and Zebulon. Yet it is not too far from Sepphoris which at that time was the administrative centre and the locale of a good deal of building which engaged workmen from the neighbourhood. Its inhabitants were considered illiterate and uncouth and hence were despised. 'Can anything good come out of Nazareth?' (Jn 1:46). The name of this village does not even occur in the Old Testament. Yet, God chose someone who lived in this remote village, demonstrating once again that his choices are not based on human criteria, and 'my ways are not your ways' (Is 55:8), because 'he has exalted those of low degree and the rich he has sent empty away' (Lk 1:52).[5]

'...to a virgin betrothed to a man whose name was Joseph'

We know from Luke's gospel that Mary was betrothed to a man whose name was Joseph of the house of David. The betrothal was a formal and juridical commitment which normally took place twelve months before the couple began to live together. Mary must have reflected seriously on the demands of marriage which for every Jewish woman was unquestioned. By the fact that she gave her consent, she must have assessed and appreciated in Joseph those qualities that made him a compatible husband for her. Her choice speaks of Mary's affective maturity which was the fruit of a great spiritual sensitivity itself refined by the religiosity of the true Israelite and by the actions of that God of Israel who, by entering into covenant with his people, had dealt with tender love and demanding care with those who had a special part to play in his salvific plan. Taking all this and the qualities of life of a young girl in a rural society into account, one comes to appreciate the human maturity of a woman who, though young in years, had learned a good deal about life, and who knew how to act in relationship with other members of the family and with a future husband.

'...and the virgin's name was Mary.'
In biblical terms to be known by name means that the person becomes aware that God the almighty makes himself especially present to a human being. The person becomes conscious that God is tenderly close, enfolding the person with love. This is the kind of experience that Abraham went through when God changed his name. Moses lived it when he heard God calling 'Moses, Moses'. These people were overwhelmed and felt the need of silently prostrating themselves before the One who knew them and called them by name. They were conscious that they were standing on holy ground (cf. Gen 17:5; Ex 3:4-5). But they also opened their hearts because of the familiarity with which they were addressed. So too with Mary who experienced being tenderly wrapped by God's love and who marvelled.

And (the Angel Gabriel) went in and said
'Rejoice, so highly favoured!' (Lk 1:28, JB)

When applied to a spiritual being, the phrase
'went in' does not refer to a local movement and
presence, but to an inner action of God in the spirit
of the person through which God communicates
with the person. In this case God was increasingly
and powerfully making Mary aware of his special
presence, of his unique and personal love for her.
Such an experience could only bring about joy.
Hence in the account Mary related that she
perceived a quiet invitation to rejoice because she
was 'filled with grace'. The Greek verb expresses
great intensity and profusion, and is used here in
the passive voice. Thus the evangelist highlights
Mary's perception of receiving God's overwhelming
and gratuitous love. The verb also indicates that
Mary had been filled with grace because she had
been the object of a constant and prolonged activity
of God. He filled her with his grace and acted in her
with his fashioning touch like a jeweller who
constantly refines the precious object of his art and
covers it with gold.[6] It was the awareness of this
intense love of God that fostered in her great
interior joy: 'Sing aloud, O daughter of Zion; shout,
O Israel! Rejoice and exult with all your heart, O
daughter of Jerusalem! The King of Israel, the Lord,
is in your midst' (Zeph 3:14-15).

God's promises of his presence among his people
are being fulfilled. Mary was overwhelmed by this
keen perception of God's nearness in all-embracing
love, and thus rejoiced.

'... the Lord is with you!' (Lk 1:28)

Such a special closeness of God, however, gradually developed in Mary an awareness that he was asking something of her, that he was entrusting her with a task, a role , a mission. We have evidence of this in the account itself; the next phrase summarises an experience which obviously extended over a long period of time. The expression, 'The Lord is with you' echoes the terms used by those people whom God had chosen to accomplish a mission in salvation history. In religious and rabbinical traditions this expression had acquired a specific meaning: it had become the way to manifest what some people realised when they became aware not only of God's personal love for them, but that such a special closeness ensued from his having called them to himself in order to entrust them with a task to be performed in his name for the sake of the people. The task was not easy and therefore demanded his special nearness: 'I am with you.' Mary, who was so familiar with the stories of the patriarchs and prophets, knew the meaning of this expression which had been used in the accounts of their vocations. It is not surprising that having interiorly experienced something which resembled these accounts the same formula would have been used when recounting the story of her own progressive growth in the discovery of her vocation. By this phrase, then, Mary conveyed that at a given point in life she became conscious that if God had established a very special relationship with her, this was with a view to a mission which was going to be difficult and very demanding.

> She was deeply disturbed by these words and
> asked herself what this greeting could mean
> (Lk 1:29, JB).

Having become aware that God was manifesting
his special love for her, that he was especially close,
and that he was demanding something of her, Mary
was naturally 'deeply disturbed', and she asked
herself what all of this could mean. In the tradition
of the patriarchs and prophets she knew that God
was about to ask of her something that went
beyond human capacities. Hence, she spent time
'considering in her mind' (Lk 2:29) what this special
communication by God might mean and imply.
Mary knew well that the divinely-wrought joy of
her relationship with God and his action in her
would, once it was evident, be challenged to the
core by her family and her society. She was giving
God her body, her reputation and perhaps even her
life: such were the realities and the moral codes
which bound the life of her people. As she spent
time pondering, the angel of the Lord reassured
Mary and thus fostered in her the interior calm
which she needed in order to listen to God's
communication.

> Do not be afraid, for God has been gracious to
> you (Lk 1:30).

These phrases also echo the experiences of the
patriarchs and prophets who, in their bewilderment
and apprehension, had to be calmed in order to be
plunged into the mystery of God and his saving
will. Abraham, Moses, Isaiah, Jeremiah and many

others perceived words of reassurance that come ultimately and only through the awareness that one is the object of God's favour and thus is held securely in God's hands. It was in this way that Mary gradually became calm and thus capable of listening to that God who speaks quietly and can be heard only when there is stillness in the heart. She could then abandon herself to that all-embracing love of God.

> And behold, you will conceive in your
> womb and bear a son, and you shall call
> his name Jesus... (Lk 1:31).

Mary was told that she was meant to conceive and bear a son, but simultaneously she was told the name that must be given to this child. In Jewish tradition it was the father who chose the name, yet the father of this child is not a man but God himself. By telling Mary what the name of the child must be, God the Father expresses who this child will be: 'Jesus'. The significance of this name is made explicit in Matthew's account to Joseph, Mary's husband: '...he will save his people from their sins' (Mt 1:21). The child, then, is the long-awaited Messiah, and Mary is made conscious that her vocation is to be the mother of the saviour.

> He will be great, and will be called the Son of
> the Most High; and the Lord will give to him
> the throne of his father, David,
> and he will reign over the house of Jacob
> forever;

and of his kingdom there will be no end (Lk
1:32-33).

In a progressive way Mary was led to understand
ever more clearly the implications of that name
"Jesus." Because of her familiarity with the core of
Jewish tradition rooted in the messages of the
prophets who were looking hopefully to the messianic times, Mary intuitively grasped the relevance
of the messianic titles which referred to the one
who was meant to be her son. In later years, when
Jesus had already accomplished his mission and
had returned to his Father, she could see clearly
how the messianic prophecies had been fulfilled in
him. When as a young woman she had been
invited to collaborate with God and to become the
mother of such a son, she had grasped under God's
action that the one she was asked to bear was not
the triumphant Messiah who would conquer with
power and might, but the humble servant of
Yahweh. She understood that God was asking her
to be the mother of the true Messiah whom devout
Israel was expecting, the Messiah that Isaiah had
presented as the Suffering Servant.

> ...he had no form or comeliness
> that we should look at him,
> and no beauty that we should desire him.
> He was despised and rejected by men;
> a man of sorrows, and acquainted with grief;
> and as one from whom men hide their faces
> he was despised, and we esteemed him not.
> Surely he has borne our griefs

and carried our sorrows;
yet we esteemed him stricken,
smitten by God, and afflicted.
But he was wounded for our transgressions,
he was bruised for our iniquities;
upon him was the chastisement that made us
whole,
and with his stripes we are healed (Is 53:2b-5).

One can gather what must have gone through the heart of this young woman when she was presented with the invitation to be become the mother of the Saviour, but a saviour who had to suffer. Yet because of her openness to God and her readiness to do what God requested of her, Mary simply asked God, 'How can this be since I have no husband?' (Lk 1:34). She was a virgin, and as such she had true and total openness to God, that is, a total capacity to receive. But in her case the capacity to receive from a human being what would make her a mother had been reserved exclusively for God. She had centred her life on God, and she had offered the whole of her being to him in virginity.

In keeping with the expectations and traditions of her family she had consented to be betrothed to Joseph. In God's providence this marriage was the way in which God himself would protect her and her reputation as well as that of the child-to-be by putting at her side a companion who, in his turn, by having responded to his vocation to virginity, was capable of exercising the functions of a father towards a child who was conceived by the power of the Almighty.

Mary's question was obviously aimed at knowing how she could enter into God's plan, and God himself graciously satisfied her need to understand how she could become a mother while being a virgin. The answer to that crucial dilemma is given to Mary in very clear terms:

> The Holy Spirit will come upon you, and the power of the Most High will overshadow you; therefore the child to be born will be called holy, the Son of God (Lk 1:35).

The Spirit which is life and the bond of love between Father and Son would descend upon Mary so that the power of God himself would enfold and permeate her to make fruitful her virginal womb and make her the virgin mother of Jesus.

As in the case of so many others who had been called for a special mission which demanded complete trust in the power of God, he graciously gave to Mary a sign of confirmation: 'your kinswoman Elizabeth in her old age has also conceived a son' (Lk 1:36). Mary knew that 'with God nothing will be impossible' (Lk 1:37).

> And Mary said, 'Behold, I am the handmaid of the Lord; let it be to me according to your word' (Lk 1:38).

Through this process of growth in understanding God's plan and the role she was to play so that it could be fulfilled, Mary was led to a degree of maturity in her relationship with God that enabled her to say 'I am the handmaid of the Lord...'. It is thus that 'the Word became flesh' (Jn 1:14). As a virgin whose heart had been fashioned and moulded by God so as to be totally his, she had become aware of a special nearness of God to her — a presence from within — because God was dwelling in her. However, at the moment of the conception of Jesus, it was not only the indwelling of God in a human being, but the Incarnation of the Son of God taking flesh from her and being alive in her. As every woman, Mary experienced the incredible joy and wonder of the new life pulsating in her, to which she herself was conveying life. Yet the amazement for Mary was immeasurably intensified because her child was the Son of the Heavenly Father. The conception of Jesus was not only the indwelling of God in a human being, but the incarnation of the Son of God taking flesh from her and being alive in her in his humanity. God's love was so personal and so concrete that it moved from the realm of spiritual experience to love's most sublime physical result: the conception of a child. She knew that what was happening in her and to her — body and spirit — which heralded motherhood were nothing less than expressions of God's overwhelming love.

The relevance of 'in and through' Mary can be more adequately appreciated when one considers that 'in her' implies maternity and all it entails, that is, a maternity of a body that will be given up for the sake of humanity so 'that they may have life' (Jn 10:10). 'Through her' implies a deliberate response to an invitation that obviously entailed a difficult

33

situation in the family and the society that surrounded her and also in the long-range living out of her motherhood at the side of a son who was rejected and sentenced to death.

* * *

Following what Mary shared about her gradual growth in understanding God's ways and about her acquiescence in God's will which enabled the Son of God to be conceived in her, we have the account of an episode which reveals a further development of her vocation. The Son was being formed in her womb. The Son of God who was coming into this world to serve and not to be served was already uniting Mary to himself in this attitude of service which was the hallmark of this messiahship.

> In those days Mary arose and went with haste into the hill country, to a city of Judah, and she entered the house of Zechariah and greeted Elizabeth (Lk 1:39-40).

Mary's readiness to rise and go, and the inner urge to be close to someone who needed her highlight another aspect of her personality: she was attentive to what was happening in and around her. And so she promptly left Nazareth in Galilee to go to Judaea where her cousin Elizabeth was soon to give birth to the one whose mission was to prepare the way of the Lord, Mary's own son. We do not know the route that Mary followed to reach Judaea; was it through the hills and valleys of Samaria? Was it along the Jordan river on the road of the kings (the route preferred by most Jews travelling to Jerusalem)? It is not relevant to know which way she went, but it is important to ponder the speed of her response to the promptings of the same Spirit who animated the One whom she carried in her womb. Her response entailed her willingness to face the hardships, fatigue and danger of a long journey. Such a decision could have been made only by a mature woman accustomed to carrying out her responsibilities selflessly.

When greeted by Elizabeth, who voiced her surprise that the mother of her Lord should come to her, Mary reacted with utter simplicity, expressing her own self-image: a lowly and little 'handmaid' of God, conscious nevertheless of God's liberality and gratuitous generosity to those who realise their utter dependence on God. In giving voice to her own sentiments, Mary selected those traditional descriptions which speak of the way the Messiah would come, not in might and splendour, but in lowliness and servanthood.

> AndMary remained with her [Elizabeth] about three months, and returned to her home (Lk 1:56).

This is a very simple, factual statement, but the words hide the actual accomplishment of a multitude of humble tasks performed with gentleness and delicacy for an older woman who had become a mother.

Meanwhile, what was going on in the mind and

heart of Joseph, Mary's betrothed? Had he already become aware that Mary was expecting a child? Was Mary holding the secret in her heart, a secret that in one way or another Joseph would have to know? What did Mary experience while Joseph was considering what to do? Her esteem for Joseph must have intensified the poignancy of her acceptance of God's plan. In the text there is simple silence, though perhaps the psalmist gives a clue to Mary's sentiments:

> God is our refuge and strength
> a very present help in trouble...
> God is in the midst of her,
> she shall not be moved;
> God will help her right early (Ps 46:1,5).

Once Joseph had made his decision to accept her into his home, Mary serenely and securely entrusted herself to him. The power of the Most High had overshadowed Mary and she had conceived. She was the true mother of God's Son, a son given to her as a true mother. She and her child were entrusted to Joseph, her divinely-appointed companion who had been refined by God to live with her their total belonging to God and their dedication to the mission he had confided to them. By such a spiritual and affective bond, which had its roots in God's eternal plan, Mary knew that they could and would create the atmosphere that would be the suitable environment for the Son of God made man to grow. Such a bond which would be lived without conjugal relations would nevertheless be rich in that mutuality which fosters true warmth in a home.

While Mary was carrying the child in her womb, and Joseph was becoming ever more keenly aware that he was to act as the shadow of the Father, they were united in a response to what had become a common vocation.

3

The Vocation of Mary and Joseph

Once Mary and Joseph were together in Joseph's home, they must have shared with one another what each had gone through in the previous months. Mary must have told Joseph something about her experience of God's nearness and of God's invitation to become a mother while remaining a virgin. Joseph must have told Mary about his painful bewilderment when he learned that she was with child before they lived together. Perhaps they shared with each other their recognition that her child was to be the person in whom the messianic titles would find fulfilment. They must have endeavoured in whatever ways possible to help each other to grow in awareness of what God intended to do, each helping the other to grasp and to respond to the implications of what they had surrendered to. The uniqueness of their vocation did not remain a 'state' to be accepted and somehow incorporated into 'normal' village life. Indeed, soon after beginning life together, they were again called beyond their imaginations and their expectations.

And Joseph also went up from Galilee, from the city of Nazareth, to Judea, to the city of David which is called Bethlehem, because he was of the house and lineage of David, to be enrolled with Mary, his betrothed, who was with child (Lk 2: 4-5).

Our first knowledge of the life of Joseph and Mary together is their trip to Bethlehem on the occasion of a census. The uniqueness of their vocations is now assuaged by companionship. The care and support which Joseph provided to Mary, his attentiveness to her needs and her sensitivities as she awaited the birth of her child, must have eased the burdens of the journey for her. For this most unusual couple, the expectation of the child's birth mingled with their religious expectation of the Messiah and united them in wonder and the sense of the divine presence.

Because he had taken Mary into his home, Joseph was the head of a family and as such he fulfilled his civic and religious duties. He was not unmindful that one of the three most important duties of a husband in the Jewish tradition was to provide shelter for his wife. He was also an Israelite living in a country occupied by the Romans, and as such he accepted the requirements of the civil authorities. The religious overtones of Joseph's response are found in his return to Bethlehem because he was a descendant of the house of David. Joseph's responsibilities, then, went from the lofty ones of his Davidic ancestry to the practical ones of finding lodging.[1]

Like Abraham (cf. Gen 12: 1-9), Joseph set out on a journey, making his way stage by stage through mountains and desert, caring for a pregnant wife who (if one conflates the narratives) was travelling to Judaea for the second time in nine months. We can imagine his care and concern for her as they faced the hazards of travel when she was near the end of her pregnancy. Then, having survived the ordeal of the journey, Joseph's caring was even more severely tested when there was no room for them in the inn. How difficult it must have been for Joseph to bring Mary into the roughness and brutality of a Middle Eastern caravanserai, knowing her own sensitivities and their need for privacy. Perhaps they saw one of the many natural caves in the area as a real refuge!

In this whole episode, Mary and Joseph responded to the God who acts through human mediators. Joseph undoubtedly acted with a mature sense of responsibility, trying to do what was best for his wife in very demanding circumstances.

> While they were there the time came for her to have her child, and she gave birth to a son, her first-born (Lk 2: 6-7, JB).

> ... And in that region there were shepherds out in the field, keeping watch over their flock by night. And an angel of the Lord appeared to them:...'to you is born this day in the city of David a Saviour, who is Christ the Lord'... And they went with haste and found Mary and Joseph, and the babe lying in a manger... Mary kept all these things, pondering them in her heart (Lk 2: 8-19).

A mother and her child.... The fact that there was no room for them in the inn, a place filled with movement and noise, actually provided Mary with a more fitting setting in which to live the joy of her maternity with the unique religious quality that her being the mother of Jesus entailed.

We appropriate the evangelists' silence about Joseph's sentiments at the birth of Jesus. But the sacred writers do give us two clues to Joseph's experience. When the shepherds told of their hurried journey to Bethlehem and their encounter with this small family, 'all who heard it wondered at what the shepherds told them' (Lk 2:18). This astonishment is counter-poised by Mary's silent contemplation: she 'kept all these things, pondering them in her heart' (Lk 2:19)[2] If others 'wondered', what about Joseph? If Mary 'pondered', what about Joseph? We can justly and humbly assert that Joseph's response was similar.

Mary and Joseph witnessed the shepherds' visit and heard them relate 'the saying which had been told them concerning this child' (Lk 2:17). It was the first homage given to the child, but it was given by the 'little ones' of this world. Mary treasured and pondered...Joseph treasured and pondered.

> At the end of eight days, when he was circumcised, he was called Jesus, the name given by the angel before he was conceived in the womb (Lk 2:21).

The unity of Mary and Joseph is made explicit in their naming of the child. In the Lukan Infancy

Narrative, Mary and Joseph together name the child. The divine messages received by each of them entailed deep repercussions for the other and for their relationship; they both embraced the divine plan which involved a unique living out of marriage and parenthood. Their sharing of their vocation experiences had obviously included the important detail of the child's name. Now they acted together to name the child as they have been directed. At the same time, the name they give leads them to grasp more fully who Jesus is, and therefore what their roles and relationship to each other and to Jesus will be. Their rootedness in Scripture and their openness to the divine enabled them gradually to assimilate the reality and the implications of naming this child 'Jesus'. The joint reaction to what had transpired and to its implications is reflected in their response variously translated as 'marvel' and 'wonder' (Lk 2:33); in this event they shared a similar contemplative experience.

* * *

And when the time came for their purification according to the law of Moses, they brought him up to Jerusalem to present him to the Lord (as it is written in the Law of the Lord, 'every male that opens the womb shall be called holy to the Lord') and to offer a sacrifice according to what is said in the law of the Lord, 'a pair of turtledoves, or two young pigeons' (Lk 2: 22-24).

In the narrative of the presentation of the child

Jesus in the Temple, there are two series of repetitions which shed light on Mary and Joseph and their union in fulfilling their mission. The evangelist refers to Mary and Joseph collectively, as 'they' (vv. 22, 39), 'the parents' (v.27), and 'his father and mother' (v. 33). Five times in this account (vv. 22, 23, 24, 27, 29), the author notes that Joseph provided that the requirements of the Law be met with regard to Jesus.[3] Once again they are portrayed as pious but discerning Jews. For all the 'marvels' that had happened to them, they did not abandon the Law. They knew when and how to obey, and perceived themselves as under the Law even after they had encountered so intimately a God who does not always follow the Law.

Mary and Joseph had been brought up as all young members of Jewish society in an environment in which individual, familial and social life were imbued with the religious spirit rooted in the Law and the history of the Jewish people. In compliance with the divinely-given command in Leviticus (12:28) every first-born boy had to be presented to the Lord. Luke the narrator associated this event with the purification although they were two distinct prescriptions of the Law.[4]

Faithful observers of what was prescribed by the Law, Mary and Joseph fulfilled their duty of presenting the child to God in the Temple at Jerusalem. As they approached the Temple carrying Jesus, they knew that what the people of Israel had treasured during the course of their history, that is, the awareness that God was with them, was now giving way to its deepest fulfilment. The incarnate

43

Son of God was entering into the house of his Father. Jesus, Emmanuel, was present, not as a great and strong wind through the mountains, breaking the rocks into pieces, not as an earthquake, not even as fire, but as 'a still small voice' (1 K 19: 11-12).

The religious act of the presentation was accompanied by the offering of five shekels or, for those of more humble means, a pair of turtledoves. The significance of such an offering was that the first-born son had to be redeemed. This child had no need of redemption; in fact, he had come to redeem humankind, to save his people from their sins. Mary and Joseph had become increasingly conscious of who Mary's child was and what his destiny was going to be, so that when they performed this ritual they moved towards the altar in a spirit of oblation. They were presenting and offering to the Father the child who was so dear to them, Mary's first-born and only son.

> Now there was a man in Jerusalem, whose name was Simeon and this man was righteous and devout; looking for the consolation of Israel, and the Holy Spirit was upon him (Lk 2:25).

While Mary and Joseph were in the Temple, an old man named Simeon, 'a righteous and devout person', deeply united to God, came to them. He was a true Israelite who had longingly fixed the eyes of his heart on the Messiah to come. Because he was open to the lights of God, the Holy Spirit had revealed to him that he would not die before seeing the promised Saviour with his own eyes. Simeon approached the parents 'as they brought in the child Jesus', reverently took him in his arms and expressed what was welling up in his heart. Now he was ready for death because his expectations had been transformed into present reality: 'Now Master, you can let your servant go in peace' (Lk 2:29, JB).

Simeon recognised in Jesus the One who had been announced by the prophets as the Saviour of humanity. He realised that in Jesus God's salvation embraces not only God's people Israel, but it also encircles the nations: 'I will make you the light of the nations, so that my salvation may reach to the ends of the earth' (Is 49:6, JB).

After blessing them, Simeon addressed Mary. His words impacted her whole being as if she were being pierced through. They brought about an ever-firmer grasp of the reality of her Son and therefore of her own vocation and mission. Simeon put into relief the bond that existed between the mission of this child and that of his mother when he declared to her, 'This child is set for the fall and rising of many in Israel' (Lk 2:34). He thus prophetically announced how the Messiah would fulfil his mission as the Suffering Servant. At the same time Simeon highlighted in very vivid terms that Mary would have to suffer in order to be close to her Son as he accomplished his mission. Joseph listened, and silently stood at her side.

> ...the angel of the Lord appeared to Joseph in a dream and said, 'Rise, take the child and his

> mother, and flee to Egypt, and remain there
> till I tell you; for Herod is about to search for
> the child, to destroy him' (Mt 2:13).

This dream reminds us of the way God communicated with Abraham: 'Leave your country... and your father's house, for the land I will show you...' (Gen 12:1,JB). Joseph was also led, in faith, to a foreign land with no certainty about the future. The difficulty of Joseph's mission was becoming increasingly evident. He had to escape with his wife. They had to leave hastily and take the child to Egypt. They had to leave what was familiar to them and move into the unknown in all possible ways. In all this, moreover, Joseph the builder, from an insignificant village, was responsible for the life of the infant Messiah which was threatened by the seemingly all-powerful Herod. Yet there is no mention here of any hesitation on Joseph's part; rather, there was immediacy in his response: 'And he rose' (Mt 2:14).

> After Herod's death an angel of the Lord
> appeared in a dream to Joseph in Egypt and
> said, 'Get up, take the child and his mother
> with you, and go back to the land of Israel...'
> (Mt 2:19, JB).

After Herod's death there was another divine intervention through which Joseph and Mary were told how to continue their mission. Joseph, in his docility to God, 'got up' and together with Mary responded immediately and exactly. Their understandable human perplexity about what to do and their fears for the sake of the child were dispelled by God's action in Joseph: '... being warned in a dream he withdrew to the district of Galilee. And he went and dwelt in a city called Nazareth' (Mt 2:22-23). We are told by the evangelist that this going to Nazareth was so '... that what was spoken through the prophets might be fulfilled, "He shall be called a Nazarene"' (Mt 2:23).

> They returned into Galilee, to their own city, Nazareth. And the child grew and became strong, filled with wisdom... (Lk 2:39-40).

While Mary and Joseph were in exile, away from their families, they had to be fully supportive of one another. Their relationship had obviously deepened. The concern they shared for the child have undoubtedly bound them even more closely together. The return to their home country must have brought a certain relief: the child would now be able to grow in that social setting which was so congenial to them. And yet there was also a question: How would they be looked upon after a prolonged absence in a foreign land? How would the child be regarded, this child who was their secret?

Mary and Joseph took up their roles as parents. The concise statement about their life in Nazareth gives significant information about their life over a long period. Mary and Joseph had complementary roles in Jesus' upbringing. Like all mothers, Mary would have been occupied with all the processes included in making bread and preparing food, with gathering wood and water, and with making and maintaining their clothing. When he was a little boy, Jesus would have spent time with her while she did these tasks.

As he became more independent as a child, he would have spent more time with Joseph, who was responsible for his education and the preparation of his trade. Joseph was a builder, and his piety would have led him to follow the rabbinical injunction to teach his son a trade; Jesus was introduced into his foster-father's building trade. Believed to be the son of Joseph and socially accepted as such, Jesus did not disdain to be identified with Joseph the just man who was a builder.[5] Joseph's provision for Jesus' education in Judaism would have begun with the lessons in reading Scripture provided at the local synagogue and would probably have continued with training or tutoring by regional rabbis. Thus Jesus' wisdom was nurtured by the inherent wisdom of his parents who brought him up in a village context in which weekly synagogue reading and discussion of the Torah, the prophets and the sapiential books were supplemented by Galilean religious and social contacts.

The setting for Jesus' growth was a small village where life was routine to the point of a monotony that was broken only by religious feasts and pilgrimages and the occasional arrival of traders, minstrels, wonder-workers. It was a life of hard physical labour to provide basic daily necessities in a social situation characterised as 'adequate sufficiency'.[6] In such a situation Jesus grew to maturity at the side of a man and a woman whose wisdom was rooted in the wisdom of God revealed in the Scriptures. Prayer and the realities of the daily life of an average craftsman's family in a peasant society would have deepened this wisdom.

* * *

> Now his parents went to Jerusalem every year at the feast of Passover. And when he was twelve years old, they went up according to custom. . . (Lk 2: 41-51).

One of the major events that interrupted ordinary life was the annual pilgrimage to Jerusalem for the feast of the Passover.[7] We are told that Mary and Joseph went 'as usual' (JB), and that Jesus, on this occasion of his approaching adulthood, accompanied them. The introductory statement of this episode echoes two items previously emphasised in the Lukan gospel: Mary and Joseph are linked together as Jesus' parents (Lk 2: 41, 43, 48, 51), and they are portrayed as devoted to the Law (Lk 2:41).

On this occasion, however, at the end of the first day's return journey, Mary and Joseph could not find Jesus among the members of their caravan. Objectively this does not indicate any failure on their part, because the normal mode of travel was in a company or caravan in which a whole village or extended family travelled together. The supposition that Jesus was with his kinsfolk was completely congruous. But the anxiety and shock experienced by Mary and Joseph when they could not find Jesus were not only those of ordinary parents in a similar situation; their concern was intensified by their shared history. How gruelling those three days of searching 'everywhere' must have been for them who had so conscientiously protected Jesus when he had been threatened after his birth. With what pangs they must have searched for him! Had he been caught in a riot and been injured or even captured by Roman soldiers? Were Herod's still-powerful and conniving allies even now threatened by the boy-king of the previous decade? Had Jesus been kidnapped? How their imagination must have tortured them those three days when successive possibilities led to nothing.

The deep bond between Mary and Joseph in their caring for the child is manifest in Mary's statement: '... your father and I have been looking for you anxiously' (Lk 2:48).[8] Neither parent had been paralysed by fear and darkness; together they had acted, together they had searched.

When at long last they found him, it was in the Temple, '... sitting among the teachers, listening to them and asking them questions; and all who heard him were amazed at his understanding and his answers' (Lk 2: 46-7). The evangelist does not mention the relief of Mary and Joseph, only their astonishment. For a second time this child of Galilee has been singled out in the Temple. Mary poured out the motions gripping Joseph and herself: 'Why?' Her question gives a hint of how she and Joseph had educated Jesus: they expected him to have a motive for his actions; they drew out of him an explanation for his behaviour. In true rabbinical fashion, Jesus responded to a question with a question; Jesus too, fostered growth in them by questioning, by drawing the ones known as his parents to a deeper faith, to an ever more radical response to their vocations as mother and stepfather of the Messiah. He pointed to his total allegiance to the heavenly Father, to the totality of the Father's will, to his own mission as the 'One who is sent'.

Jesus' response to Mary and Joseph was uttered when he was on the brink of manhood, taking his place as an adult member of the Jewish community. The joyous relief of reunion was muted by Jesus' bittersweet announcement to his parents that he would inevitably pass from their care to his being totally of the heavenly Father and totally for the heavenly Father. Yet no matter what their lack of understanding or their need to step back from Jesus' emerging adulthood, they returned to Nazareth as a family, the family of Joseph the builder: Jesus 'lived under their authority' (Lk 2:51, JB).

4

The Fulfilment of the Mission

The years spent by Jesus 'under the authority' of
Mary and Joseph were years of growth. He grew in
age, wisdom and grace (Lk 2:40, 52). Mary and
Joseph played their respective and delicate roles in
the formation of the humanity of Christ, whose
refinement is made manifest in the way he dealt
with people during his ministry. The years that
Mary, Joseph and Jesus spent in Nazareth, a tiny
Galilean village bordering the territory of Zebulon
were years of preparation.

As Joseph the builder travelled back and forth
from Sepphoris, perhaps in the company of the boy
Jesus, did the words of Isaiah echo in his mind?

> Land of Zebulon! Land of Naphtali!
> Way of the sea on the far side of the Jordan,
> Galilee of the nations!...
> on those who dwell in the land and shadow
>   of death
> a light has dawned. (Mt 4: 14-16, JB; cf. Is 9:1)

Had he not pondered what Simeon had voiced
years before when he and Mary were presenting the
Child in the Temple:

> 'Mine eyes have seen thy salvation which

thou hast prepared in the presence of all
peoples, a light for revelation to the Gentiles
and for glory to thy people Israel' (Lk 2:30-
32).

Joseph does not disappear from the gospels at the
end of the Infancy Narratives. Luke opens his
genealogy in this manner: 'Jesus, when he began his
ministry, was about thirty years of age, being the
son (as was supposed) of Joseph...' (Lk 3:23). And
Matthew describes the people's astonishment when
Jesus taught in Nazareth in these terms: 'Is not this
the carpenter's son?' (Mt 13:55). What did it mean
that Jesus, the Word Incarnate, allowed himself to
be designated as 'the carpenter's son'? We can
presume that Jesus did not disdain to be identified
with Joseph, the just man. Joseph had no idols, but
had obeyed God alone. He had lived out the Law in
his life, but had known how to go beyond the Law
when God called. Joseph was a person who
followed wherever God led him. Joseph was also
ready to respond to God's plan and give himself
completely to that plan. He embraced a vocation to
virginity, and his virginal heart allowed him to be
open, merciful and caring towards Mary, not using
her or treating her as his culture sometimes treated
women.

But beyond Jesus' identification with Joseph is
the reality that when Jesus came to express his
experience of God, he used the name he had used
for Joseph, 'Abba'.[1] For many years, whenever
Jesus had used that familial word, he had meant

'Joseph'. From among all the images of God that Jesus had learned in his life as a pious Jew, he applied the familiar name of his foster-father to his God, his heavenly Father.

The final appearance of Joseph in the gospels is on the occasion when Jesus first voiced his total commitment to the will of the Father in heaven and thus to the mission that he had received from him. This announcement heralded the last phase of Joseph's mission: he effaced himself to leave Jesus entirely to his only true Father. Joseph is lost in the One whose shadow he had been. In using the word 'Abba' for that true Father, Jesus uttered the ultimate epithet for Joseph.

* * *

Our information about Mary is not as limited as that which is given about Joseph. There are several episodes in which she was present after Jesus left Nazareth and 'went about all Galilee, teaching in their synagogues and preaching the gospel of the kingdom and healing every disease and every infirmity among the people' (Mt 4:23). We see her at the wedding feast which took place at Cana, manifesting a new aspect of her motherhood, her care for people.[2] We find her at Capharnaum looking for her son, and on that occasion we hear why Jesus loved her so much: she was the woman who had always 'listened to the Word of God', and while treasuring that Word, she also lived it out.

Then, when Jesus' 'hour' came, we find Mary at the foot of the Cross. It was there that Jesus' love for his mother manifested itself: she was the last person on earth he thought of and cared for, entrusting her to his Beloved Disciple.

Yet, while doing so, he asked her to continue the mission that she had so lovingly and firmly accomplished in his regard. Mary was to take as her children the men and women who will believe in Jesus. But so that they may be best brought to the life of her unique Son, she had to go still further and to be totally united to the Father in that love which led him to deliver his Son for the salvation of the world. [3]

'For God so loved the world that he gave his only Son' (Jn 3:16). In full union with the will of the Father and thus accomplishing her mission, Mary stood at the foot of the Cross and offered her Son to the Father so that people may have life. So much did Mary love the world as to give her only son. The will of Mary was then totally conformed to the will of the Father. Mary is completely lost in the all-embracing love that God has for humankind.

Notes

Chapter 1: The Vocation of Joseph

1. Scripture quotes are from the Revised Standard Version unless indicated 'JB' (the *Jerusalem Bible*).

2. For a description of first-century Jewish village society, see for example: Bruce J. Malina, *The New Testament World: Insights from Cultural Anthropology.* Atlanta: John Knox, 1981, chapters 1 and 2; Sean Freyne, *Galilee, Jesus and the Gospels: Literary Approaches and Historical Investigations.* Philadelphia: Fortress, 1988, 152-55; *Bible Times* 1 (1988): 44-5; and Kaari Ward, et. al., eds. *Jesus and His Times.* Pleasantville, New York: Reader's Digest, 1987, *passim.*

3. The Greek word usually translated into English as 'carpenter' literally means 'builder' or 'stone mason'. See R. Batey, 'Is not this the Carpenter?' *New Testament Studies* 30 (1984): 24-58; Paul Hanley Furfey, 'Christ as Tekton', *Catholic Biblical Quarterly* 17 (April 1955): 324-35; and *Bible Times,* 42.

On the significance of Sepphoris, see Shirley Case Jackson, 'Jesus and Sepphoris,' *Journal of Biblical Literature* 45 (1926): 14-22; Francis W. Boelter, 'Sepphoris: Seat of the Galilean Sanhedrin', *Explor* 3:1 (winter 1977): 36-43.

4. Benedict T. Viviano, 'The Gospel According to Matthew' in *The New Jerome Biblical Commentary.* Eds. Raymond E. Brown, Joseph A. Fitzmyer and Roland E. Murphy. Englewood Cliffs, New Jersey: Prentice Hall, 1990, 657:b.

5. As Raymond Brown remarks: '...Joseph understands that the Law in all its complexity allows behaviour that is sensitive'; (*A Coming Christ in Advent: Essays on the Gospel Narratives. Preparing for the Birth of Jesus (Matthew 1 and Luke 1).* Collegeville, Minnesota: Liturgical Press, 1988, 33).

6. Joseph Staissny, 'Le mariage Juif au début de l'ère chrétienne', *Le monde de la Bible,* 16: 42-3. On the exchange of consent, see Raymond E. Brown, *Birth of the Messiah: A Commentary on the Infancy Narratives in Matthew and Luke.* Garden City, New York: Doubleday, 1977, 127; and Ben Witherington III, *Women in the Ministry of Jesus: A Study of Jesus' Attitudes to Women and Their Roles as Reflected in His Earthly Life.* Society

for New Testament Studies Monograph Series, 51. Gen. ed. G.N.Stanton. Cambridge: Cambridge University Press, 1984, 3.

7. Malina, 44.

8. Brown discusses the three motivations advanced in Christian tradition for Joseph's justice: his kindness or mercy, his respect or awe for God's plan, and his obedience to the Law. Brown considers only the third motivation convincing: 'He (Joseph) was upright, but also merciful' (*Birth of the Messiah*,126-29; see also, *A Coming Christ in Advent*, 30-33.

9. On the functions of angels and dreams in the Old Testament, see Brown, *Birth of the Messiah*, 129, citing, Gen 16:7, 13 and 22:11, 14; Ex 3:2, 4; Jg 6:12, 14; Hos 12:5; Is 63:9.

10. On the one hand, Joseph's greatness is shown in his giving up the precious role of father in a culture in which fatherhood was so important to a man's identity (see, for example, Witherington, 5). On the other hand, 'Besides fatherly authority over Jesus, God also gave Joseph a share in the corresponding love. . . that has its origin in the Father "from whom every family in heaven and on earth is named" (Eph 3:15).' (John Paul II, Apostolic Exhortation *Redemptoris Custos*. London: Catholic Truth Society, 1989, no.8, p.17). '... Joseph showed Jesus "by special gift from heaven, all the natural love, all the affectionate solicitude that a father's heart can know".' (Pius XII, Radio Message to Catholic School Students in the United States of America (19 February 1958): AAS 50 (1958): 174).

11. Brown, *A Coming Christ in Advent*, 34: Viviano, 635:b.

12. That this was a true marriage is also pointed out by John Paul II: 'Analyzing the nature of marriage, both Saint Augustine and Saint Thomas always identify it with an "indivisible union of souls", a "union of hearts", and with "consent". These elements are found in an exemplary manner in the marriage of Mary and Joseph" (*Redemptoris custos*, no. 7, p.14; see note 15 of the Exhortation for references to the works of St Augustine and St Thomas).

13. 'Saint Joseph was called by God to serve the person and mission of Jesus directly through the exercise of his fatherhood ... his fatherhood is expressed concretely in his having made his life a service, a sacrifice to the redemptive mission connected with it; ... in having turned his human vocation to domestic love into a superhuman oblation of self,

an oblation of his heart and all his abilities into love placed at the service of the Messiah growing up in his house' (Paul VI, Discourse, 19 March 1966 (*Insegnamenti*, IV (1966): 110).

Chapter 2: The Vocation of Mary

1. Susan Marie Praeder, *The Word in Women's Worlds: Four Parables.* Zaccheus Studies: New Testament. Wilmington, Delaware: Michael Glazier, 1988, 18; Stanislao Loffreda. 'Nazareth à l'époque évangélique,' *Le Monde de la Bible* 16: 8-13; Ward, et. al., passim; Witherington, 4.

2. According to Witherington, 'a certain spiritual significance' was given to a woman's presence in the home: she was considered a helper, a joy, a blessing and an atonement (6; see also 2, 7-8).

3. Brown, *Birth of the Messiah*, 127; Staissny, 42-3; Witherington, 3.

4. John Paul ll refers to Mary's ordinariness as "… a presence so discreet as to pass almost unnoticed by the eyes of her contemporaries…" (Encyclical Letter, *Redemptoris Mater* Vatican City: Libreria Editrice Vaticana, 1987, no. 3, pp. 7-8).

5. Brown notes that many of the people in Matthew's genealogy were too insignificant to be mentioned in Israel's history, 'but they were significant to God as he prepared for the Messiah' (*A Coming Christ in Advent*, 13). The same divine paradox applies to Nazareth.

6. The verb used by Luke is one which ends in 'oo' (*omikron omega*) when in the first person, present tense. Such an ending signifies an action done with great intensity. The form of the verb in Lk 1:28 is the passive past participle which emphasises the way in which Mary had been 'filled by God'.

Another often-noted use of this verb form is in the Christological hymn in Philippians 2:6-11. Speaking of Christ's 'kenosis', St Paul coins a reflexive form so as to say that Christ emptied (humbled) himself beyond human comprehension.

Chapter 3: The Vocation of Mary and Joseph

1. On the duties of husbands, see for example, Witherington, 4. On the

importance to Matthew of Jesus' Davidic ancestry and therefore of Bethlehem, see Brown, *A Coming Christ in Advent*, 28.

2. Raymond Brown's translation is significant to our understanding of Mary: she 'kept with concern all these events, interpreting them in her heart' (*An Adult Christ at Christmas: Essays on the Three Biblical Christmas Stories Matthew 2 and Luke 2*. Collegeville, Minnesota: Liturgical Press, 1978, 24).

3. Ibid., 27.

4. Ibid.

5. A son was expected to follow his father's occupation and to remain in his social class. Malina, 102.

6. Freyne, 47.

7. Ibid., 97, 172, 186-7.

8. By having Mary ask the question Luke highlights relationships within the family. In a society in which women yielded to paternal dominance, it is Mary the mother who speaks; yet she begins her question by referring to Joseph.

Chapter 4: The Fulfilment of the Mission

1. On the use of 'abba' as derived from the language of small children in Palestinian Aramaic in the period before the New Testament, see Joachim Jeremias, *The Prayers of Jesus*. Philadelphia: Fortress, 1978, 58-9, 78, 97, lll.

2. John Paul II, *Redemptoris Mater*, no. 21, p. 45.

3. Cf. Jacques Guillet, *Jesus Christ Yesterday and Today: Introduction to Biblical Spirituality*. Trans. John Duggan. London: Geoffrey Chapman, 1965, 184-7, and John Paul II, *Redemptoris Mater*, no. 18, p.37 and no. 23, pp. 48-50.